# Mardi Gras

## Parades, Costumes, and Parties

*Elaine Landau*

**Enslow Publishers, Inc.**

40 Industrial Road          PO Box 38
Box 398              Aldershot
Berkeley Heights, NJ 07922   Hants GU12 6BP
USA                   UK

http://www.enslow.com

*For Jessica Garmizo*

**Library of Congress Cataloging-in-Publication Data**

Landau, Elaine.
  Mardi Gras—music, parades, and costumes, / Elaine Landau.
    p. cm. — (Finding out about holidays)
  Includes bibliographical references and index.
  ISBN 0-7660-1776-1
  1. Carnival—United States—Juvenile literature. 2. United
States—Social life and customs—Juvenile literature.  I. Title. II.
Series.
GT4180 .L36 2002
394.25-dc21
                                        2001004781

Printed in the United States of America

10 9 8 7 6 5 4 3 2 1

**To Our Readers:** We have done our best to make sure that all Internet addresses in this book were active and appropriate when we went to press. However, the author and publisher have no control over and assume no liability for the material available on those Internet sites or on other Web sites they may link to. Any comments or suggestions can be sent by e-mail to comments@enslow.com or to the address on the back cover.

Every effort has been made to locate all copyright holders of material used in this book. If any errors or omissions have occurred, corrections will be made in future editions of this book.

**Photo Credits:** AP Photo/Andrew J. Cohoon, p. 29; AP Photo/Frank Rumpenhorst, p. 17; AP Photo/Judi Bottoni, p. 36; AP Photo/Lionel Cironneau, p. 11; AP Photo/Lynne Sladky, p. 33; AP Photo/Max Nash, p. 25; AP Photo/Renzo Gostoli, p. 5; AP Photo/Russell McPhedran, p. 37; AP Photo/The Enterprise-Journal, Aaron Rhoads, p. 38; Cheryl Wells, p. 43 (all); © Corel Corporation, pp. 19, 24, 28, 30, 32, 39, 42 (background), 43 (background), 44, 45, 46, 47, 48; Courtesy of the Historic New Orleans Collection, pp. 10, 20; David Rae Morris REUTERS/Hulton/Archive, pp. 4, 18, 21, 26, 27; Enslow Publishers, pp. 8, 23; Hemera Technologies, Inc., pp. i, ii, iii; 7 (both), 12 (both), 14, 34 (all), 40 (all); Joseph Faria, p. 15; Lee Celano REUTERS/Hulton/Archive, pp. 16, 22; Michael DeMocker REUTERS/Hulton/Archive, pp. 6, 31; Quentin Massys, p. 13; Reuters/Drew Story/Archive Photos, p. 41; Vignette Publications, Inc., p. 35; www.photosforme.com, p. 9.

**Cover Photo:** Reuters/Drew Story/Archive Photos (background); David Rae Morris REUTERS/Hulton/ Archive (top inset); photosforme.com (middle inset); Cheryl Wells (bottom inset).

# CONTENTS

People in bright costumes and headdresses parade through the streets. It's Mardi Gras!

# CHAPTER 1

# What a Night!

It is after dark in New Orleans, Louisiana. In the middle of a crowded street, music fills the air. People all around are dancing.

A parade is coming down the street. The people in the parade are called maskers. They are all wearing masks and great costumes. Some costumes are made of brightly colored material. Many are decorated with sparkling beads or feathers. Several maskers wear huge gold hats called headdresses. Others wear green or purple headdresses.

The maskers ride on large, colorful floats.

## CARNIVAL IN BRAZIL

*One of the most famous Mardi Gras celebrations in the world occurs every year in Rio de Janero, Brazil. In Brazil as well as in other countries around the world, this celebration is called Carnival.*

5

During Mardi Gras, everyone tries to catch the beads and coins people toss to them from balconies or floats.

The floats look like small stages on wheels. They are slowly pulled by tractors.

On one float, people are riding a large golden dragon. On another, a man and a woman are dressed like a king and a queen. Their royal helpers are with them. There is also a large white horse made of plaster. The horse is covered with roses and other flowers. Everything on the float sparkles. The night sky seems to light up.

**Can you imagine being crowned king or queen of the Mardi Gras parade?**

Lots of people watching the parade wear costumes, too. Everyone is happy and laughing. This is a night for fun. The crowd calls out to the maskers. People yell, "Throw me something, Mister."

The maskers toss small gifts from their

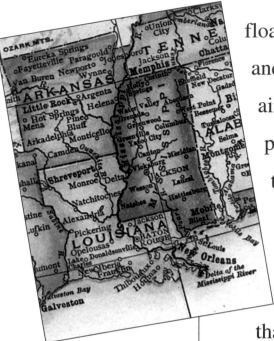

The most famous Mardi Gras parties in the United States are held in New Orleans, Louisiana.

floats to the people watching. Hard candies and small plastic Frisbees fly through the air. People are wearing the strings of plastic beads that have been tossed to them. They quickly scoop up colorful coins from the street. These have also been thrown by people on the floats. Some parade watchers take home more than memories. They bring shopping bags for all the things being tossed to them.

These last few days have been great. There were parties and wonderful meals. But the parade was the best part. No one will ever forget this magical evening. It was not a dream. It was Mardi Gras (MAR dee GRAH).

Mardi Gras is a very special holiday. There is no other day quite like it. Holidays are celebrated in many different ways. There are parades every July 4. Thanksgiving Day dinners are fun. New Year's Eve is known for its parties. And on Halloween people wear costumes.

But Mardi Gras is the only holiday when all these things are done. It is a time for make-believe and for having fun. It is also a time for good food and good friends. People come together from all over the country to celebrate Mardi Gras. It is like no other time of the year.

In the United States, Mardi Gras is celebrated in some areas of the South. Many of these places are near the Gulf of Mexico. A few of the larger Mardi Gras celebrations are in New Orleans, Louisiana; Mobile, Alabama; and Galveston, Texas. But the holiday is celebrated in other places, too.

The colors of Mardi Gras are purple, green, and gold.

9

People have always enjoyed dressing up for Mardi Gras balls.

# CHAPTER 2

# Not a New Holiday

**CARNIVAL IN FRANCE**

*A large Carnival celebration is held every year in Nice, which is in the French Riviera. Everyone attends parties, parades, and masquerade balls.*

The Mardi Gras holiday started hundreds of years ago in Europe. Celebrating Mardi Gras was a way to welcome spring. People saw spring as a new beginning. They danced and sang and feasted. Everyone hoped for a happy year ahead. They hoped for good crops and healthy farm animals.

Mardi Gras is always held on the Tuesday before Lent. Lent is an important time for Christians. It is not a celebration. It is a time for prayer. People ask for forgiveness for their sins.

Lent lasts for six weeks. For many years

Christians gave up meat, cheese, and butter during Lent. People often fasted, which means not eating at all.

Mardi Gras is the last feast day before Lent begins. It is a day for eating good food and for having fun. Mardi Gras is French for "Fat Tuesday." Perhaps the name comes from the custom of a fat ox being paraded through the streets during Mardi Gras.

Mardi Gras does not fall on the same day each year. The holiday can be on any Tuesday from February 3 to March 9. But it is always forty-seven days before Easter.

In some places, Mardi Gras is called Carnival. The word carnival comes from the Latin words *carne vale*, meaning "farewell to meat."

**Some Christians give up eating meat, cheese, and butter during Lent.**

Mardi Gras is more than just a one-day

celebration, though. There is a whole Carnival season that begins every year on January 6. That date is also known as Twelfth Night, because it is twelve days after Christmas. Some Christians believe that the Three Wise Men visited the baby Jesus at that time.

Twelfth Night is the start of the Mardi Gras or Carnival season. That is when the parties and fun begin. The celebrating is in full swing by Mardi Gras. Then, at the stroke of midnight, the celebration is over and Lent starts.

In some parts of the United States, Mardi Gras has been celebrated for over 200 years. The French brought us this holiday. In 1699, French explorers were in the Louisiana area. They had been traveling down the Mississippi River. They stopped about sixty miles from what is now New Orleans.

The Three Wise Men are thought to have visited the baby Jesus on January 6, twelve nights after His birth. This date is known as Twelfth Night.

The French started Mardi Gras in the United States.

The date was March 3, 1699. The men missed their homes and families. They knew that Mardi Gras was being celebrated in France. So they named the spot where they stopped *Pointe du Mardi Gras* (Mardi Gras Point).

Before long, Mardi Gras was being celebrated in America, when French people settled in the area. One settlement started in Mobile, Alabama. In 1703, the new settlers held the country's first Mardi Gras celebration.

As time passed, the celebration grew. There were balls or dances. People came in costumes and masks. They danced until late at night. Mobile has been called "The City That Started It All."

Several years later, the French began a settlement in Louisiana. It was known as *Nouvelle Orleans* (New Orleans). Mardi Gras became popular there, too. In time, New Orleans would become famous for its Mardi Gras celebrations.

Meanwhile, other French settlements celebrated Mardi Gras. People looked forward to it. Today these celebrations have grown and changed. Thousands of people now enjoy Mardi Gras. Some people live in areas where there are Mardi Gras festivals. Other people are visitors. No one wants to miss the fun.

The name *Mardi Gras,* which is French for "Fat Tuesday," is believed to have come from an old custom of parading a fat ox through the streets before Lent.

Mardi Gras parades are fun to go to, especially when the people riding the floats toss beads to everyone watching!

# CHAPTER 3

# Parades

## CARNIVAL IN GERMANY

*Carnival revelers in the German town of Mainz sometimes wear huge papier-mâché heads in their festive Mardi Gras parades. These masks are known as "Schwellkoepp," which is German for swollen heads.*

In some places, entire cities have Mardi Gras parties. Sometimes the parties take place in the streets before the Mardi Gras parades begin.

Mardi Gras parades are famous. Some areas have parades throughout Mardi Gras season. Many parades are held during the day. Others are at night.

Each parade is about something or someone. The parade may be about a famous person or an important event in history. Sometimes the parade is about a well-known story or legend.

Some Mardi Gras parades are very big. They

The Krewe of Dreux in New Orleans includes a marching band. People love to hear the rhythm of the drum circle as they pass by!

may have over three thousand people. There are huge floats, too. A Mardi Gras float can be as tall as a building.

The people riding the floats wear great costumes and masks. Often there are people playing musical instruments on the floats. There are also marching bands in the parades.

But Mardi Gras parades have more than bands and floats. There may be magicians, dancers, clowns, and motorcycle riders, too.

Special Mardi Gras clubs put on the parades. In most places, these clubs are known as krewes. But in Mobile, Alabama, the groups are called Mystic Societies.

The different krewes have interesting names. Many are named after ancient gods. One is called Aphrodite. She is the goddess of love. Another krewe is called Thor. He is the god of war and thunder.

Krewes have a long history. They started in 1857, when about a half dozen young men from New Orleans formed the first one. They called it the Mistick Krewe of

Venus is the Roman goddess of love and beauty.

Comus. Comus was an ancient god of parties and good times.

The men from the first krewe built two large floats that were pulled by horses. For Mardi Gras, they dressed in costumes and masks, and waited until it was dark. Then the Mistick Krewe of Comus paraded through the streets. Their servants carried lit torches and walked next to the floats. People came out to see the parade. Everyone clapped and cheered. It was a terrific night.

In 1857, the first krewes formed in New Orleans.

In time, more krewes formed to celebrate Mardi Gras in many ways. But most krewes put on parades. Through the years, the parades became a custom. Now, when people think of Mardi Gras, they often think of wonderful parades.

Today there are many krewes in different cities. Each krewe has a captain, the krewe's leader. Others in the krewe have special roles, too. A krewe king and queen are picked each year to watch over the parade.

Usually the king and queen are members of the krewe. But some krewes offer this honor to movie stars or popular musicians.

During the festival in New Orleans, many people gather around to watch the parades.

Mardi Gras parades are about more than the fancy floats and colorful costumes. The way the maskers treat the parade watchers is important, too. In other parades, float riders just wave and smile. But in Mardi Gras parades, they also toss small items to the crowd.

These items are known as throws. Throws

**Bourbon Street in New Orleans is the most crowded during Mardi Gras. People can catch beads and coins tossed to them from balconies, or just walk around and see people in costumes and masks parading up and down the street!**

include strings of colorful plastic beads, plastic cups, small plastic Frisbees, whistles, and candies.

Small, colorful coins are always popular. The krewe's seal, or crest, may be stamped on one side of the coin. The parade's subject is on the other side.

In Mobile, Alabama, the maskers throw

moon pies, which are small round cakes. They have chocolate icing and cream inside and are wrapped in clear plastic.

The parade watchers love to bring home throws. They call out to the maskers. Some people turn an umbrella inside out and hold it up to the floats. They hope that it will be filled with throws.

Parade watchers sometimes bring special ladders that are between eight and ten feet tall. A small bench is attached to the top. Often parents put little children on the bench. They hold the ladder's sides to steady it. The child is better able to see the parade and is in a good place to catch throws.

All parades are fun. There is always a lot to see. But Mardi Gras parades may just be the best ones.

**Beaded necklaces are a popular throw.**

Great masks are an important part of Mardi Gras. The ones shown here were worn during a Carnival celebration in Venice, Italy.

# A Closer Look at Krewes

Krewes are interesting Carnival groups. Many times, exactly who is in which krewe is a secret. Yet some people are in more than one of these Carnival clubs.

All krewes are extremely busy during the Mardi Gras season. Many have a fancy ball. Sometimes people wear costumes to the ball. Other times the women wear long gowns and the men come in tuxedos. But everyone wears great masks.

The krewe's Mardi Gras king and queen are usually chosen at the ball. At some balls, the

A krewe's king and queen usually ride on the best decorated floats. This is King Proteus, from the New Orleans Krewe of Proteus.

krewe also puts on a play. The play matches the parade's theme.

Some of the newer krewes no longer have Mardi Gras balls. Instead, they have dinners at nice hotels and restaurants. The balls and dinners are only for krewe members and their guests. But the krewes want everyone to join them for the parades.

At first, krewes were only for men. However, women wanted their own Carnival clubs. So, female Mardi Gras krewes began. Today there are all kinds of krewes. There are krewes with both male and female members. There are krewes for children. There are even krewes for pets! Of course, the pet owners join, too.

Here are just a few interesting krewes:

*The Krewe of the Munchkins.* This krewe from Galveston, Texas, is for children. The members are between four and fourteen years old. About 500 munchkins are in the krewe's parade, and there are at least thirteen floats.

*The Krewe of Barkus and Meoux.* This krewe, also from Galveston, Texas, is for pets. It is run by the animal shelter. Each year, there is a parade of animals dressed in costumes.

There are mostly dogs and cats in the parade. However, sometimes monkeys, small ponies, and guinea pigs take part. The owners parade with their pets. Some people even have costumes to match their pets.

**Some krewes, like the Krewe of Barkus and Meoux, are just for pets!**

*The Mystics of Time.* In this Mobile, Alabama, krewe, there are three fire-breathing dragons that lead the Mardi Gras parade. The first dragon is 150 feet long. The next two are smaller. Maskers ride the dragon floats and toss throws to the crowd. The dragons breathe real fire and smoke.

*Phunny Phorty Phellows.* This New Orleans krewe is made up of about fifty men and women. The Phunny Phorty Phellows have a special job. They celebrate the start of the Carnival season. Each year on January 6, krewe members put on their costumes. Then they get on a streetcar decorated for Mardi Gras. The streetcar runs along a Mardi Gras parade route.

**Great costumes and masks make every parade memorable.**

*Rex.* This is probably the best-known Carnival krewe in New Orleans. Rex's long history began in 1872. Mardi Gras parades had always been at night. But Rex had the first daytime parade.

The Rex parade is on the Mardi Gras day. It is the main event. The parade has fabulous floats and great music. It is the most photographed Mardi Gras parade.

Rex came up with the official Mardi Gras colors—gold, green, and purple. Gold stands for power. Green is for faith. Purple is for justice.

Rex also gave Mardi Gras its official song,

**Rex is the best-known New Orleans krewe. The Rex parade is the main event on the day of Mardi Gras, and Rex is known as the King of Carnival.**

Live oxen are no longer used during Mardi Gras. Now, the Krewe of Rex parades one made of papier-mâché.

"If I Ever Cease to Love." The song has very silly words. It says:

*"If I ever cease to love,*
*May cows lay eggs and fish grow legs."*

The Rex parade also has the boeuf gras, or fatted ox. Many years ago, the krewe had a live ox in its parade. Now one made out of papier-mâché, which is a light, strong kind of paper mixed with glue, is used. The ox stands for the last meat eaten before Lent.

*Zulu.* The Zulu Aid and Pleasure Club is an African-American krewe. It was named after an African tribe. People look forward to this krewe's parades. There are usually more than twenty bands and many throws. The most valued throws are Zulu's hand-painted coconuts.

This dancer is from the krewe of Zulu. Thousands of people come to enjoy the music and the throws from the Zulu krewe each year.

In the country, "beggars" chase after the best Mardi Gras prize—a chicken!

# CHAPTER 5

# Mardi Gras—Country Style

**CARNIVAL IN TRINIDAD**

*For two days each year in Port-of-Spain, Trinidad, people celebrate Carnival. This celebration features the world's best steel bands and calypsos. People dance and sing all night long!*

Mardi Gras is celebrated in many different ways. People living in the country often enjoy Mardi Gras runs. A Mardi Gras run is not just a race. It is a community event.

The run begins with a group of people in costumes. They meet at a starting point. Some are on horseback. Others arrive in trucks. A few bring musical instruments.

These costumed riders stop at different homes along the way to sing and dance. In return, they ask for food. This is known as "begging." The food will be used to make

Sometimes "beggars" are given a sack of onions.

gumbo. Gumbo is a thick soup made with meat and seafood that is served over rice.

Sometimes the "beggars" are given a bag of rice or a sack of onions. Smoked sausage is another favorite. But a chicken is the best prize. Usually the homeowner sets the chicken loose and the beggars have to catch it. Some say this is the best show of all. Everything is done in fun.

By late afternoon, the costumed riders return to town. A crowd has gathered to welcome them. A second group of people makes a large pot of gumbo. No one goes home hungry.

Afterward they celebrate. A band plays and people dance. The town enjoys Mardi Gras—country style.

## Chicken and Sausage Gumbo*

One 2-1/2 lb. chicken
salt and pepper
1 lb. smoked sausage
3/4 cup flour
1 large yellow onion
2 bunches green onions
3 large tomatoes
2-1/2 quarts hot chicken stock
2 bay leaves
1/8 tsp. dried thyme
1/2 tsp. cayenne pepper
4 cups cooked rice

1. Cut the chicken into pieces and rub with salt and pepper.

2. Chop the onion and green onion.

3. Skin tomatoes, remove seeds, and chop.

4. Cut sausages into 1-inch pieces. Heat the oil in a heavy 2 gallon pot. Add the sausage and cook until brown. Remove sausage and set aside.

4. Add chicken to pot and fry golden brown until almost completely cooked. Remove chicken and set aside.

5. Add flour to pot and cook until it becomes a copper brown. Add yellow onion and green onions. Stir and cook until they begin to color. Add tomato pulp and cook 5 minutes.

6. Add chicken, sausage, bay leaves, thyme, and cayenne pepper. Stir gently.

7. Add stock and bring to a boil for 15 minutes. Partially cover and simmer for 1 hour. Serve in bowls with rice.

* Adult supervision required.

**Gumbo is a thick soup made with meat and seafood. It is served over rice.**

A king cake is a special cake made during Mardi Gras. A tiny doll is baked inside. The person whose piece of cake contains the doll is supposed to bring the next king cake.

# CHAPTER 6
# A Great Holiday

No matter how Mardi Gras is celebrated, it is a great holiday. There is so much to do. Many schools have Mardi Gras parties. The students come in costumes and play games. Everyone enjoys eating king cakes.

A king cake is a special Mardi Gras food. It is a ring-shaped cake that some people say looks like a large doughnut. But king cakes have green, purple, and gold frosting, the colors of Mardi Gras.

King cakes also have a surprise inside them. A tiny plastic baby doll is hidden in each

cake. Someone's piece will have the toy in it. That person is supposed to bring the next king cake.

Some schools have Mardi Gras dances. They pick a Mardi Gras king and queen. Often schools have their own Mardi Gras parades, too. The students dress in costumes and parade on school grounds.

Libraries and museums also celebrate Mardi Gras. Stories may be read. There are also Mardi Gras craft hours. At the Louisiana Children's Museum in New Orleans, children make Mardi Gras masks.

There are always all kinds of Mardi Gras contests. Mardi Gras beauty contests are common. Sometimes

**Schools have different events during Mardi Gras. These students (below), from the Mc Comb High School Marching Band in Missouri, performed at a retirement home on Fat Tuesday in 2001.**

Sometimes, people play special Mardi Gras games of rugby.

there are contests for the best Mardi Gras costume. A Mardi Gras poster contest for young people is also popular.

Sporting events are enjoyed at this time, as well. Some cities have Mardi Gras rugby tournaments. Rugby is a little like football. There are Mardi Gras marathons, too. A marathon is a long footrace. Each runner hopes

**Mardi Gras is a fun holiday!**

to finish first. During Mardi Gras, the finish line may be painted in green, purple, and gold.

There are usually special events on the Monday before Mardi Gras. Lots of fun festivals are held. Everything leads up to Mardi Gras—the last day of the Carnival season. Some of the best parties, contests, and dances take place then. Often there are fireworks at night.

In some cities there are parades that continue after dark. People fill the streets, and there is music everywhere. People wish the fun would never end. But at midnight, the crowds go home and the cleanup begins.

One thing is certain. Mardi Gras will be just as great next year. This holiday is always filled with fun.

**Everyone wishes the fun of Mardi Gras would never end!**

# Mardi Gras Craft Project

★

## Mardi Gras Mask

*It does not matter where you live—anyone can catch the spirit of Mardi Gras! Making a Mardi Gras mask is a fun way to get in the spirit.*

*You will need:*

✔ **Construction paper**

✔ **Popsicle sticks**

✔ **White glue**

✔ **Safety Scissors**

✔ **Glitter, sequins, feathers, or other decorations**

**1.** Draw a pattern on the construction paper big enough to cover your eyes. It can be in the shape of a cat, a bird, or anything you like.

**2.** Use the safety scissors to carefully cut alone the lines you drew. Make sure that the holes for the eyes are big enough that you can see clearly out of them.

**3.** Turn your mask over to the back and use the white glue to attach the popsicle stick to the mask. This will be your handle.

**4.** When the glue dries, turn the mask back over and use the sequins, glitter, and feathers to decorate it. Make it as colorful as possible. When the glue dries, you can use the mask for your own Mardi Gras fun!

# Mardi Gras Craft Project

★

Let's get ready to start!

All done!

Ready for Mardi Gras!

**\*Safety Note:** Be sure to ask for help from an adult, if needed, to complete this project.

# Words to Know

★

**boeuf gras**—A fatted ox or bull. It stands for the last meat eaten before Lent begins.

**captain**—The leader of a Carnival club.

**king cake**—A ring-shaped Mardi Gras cake with gold, purple, and green icing.

**krewe**—A Carnival club or group. Krewes often have Mardi Gras parades.

**maskers**—The costumed riders on Mardi Gras floats.

**papier-mâché**—A light, strong kind of paper mixed with glue that can be used to make things.

# Words to Know

★

**rugby**—A type of football game that includes kicking, dribbling, and passing the ball in addition to tackling other players.

**throws**—Small objects that are thrown to the crowd during Mardi Gras parades.

# Reading About

★

Ancona, George. *Carnival*. San Diego, Calif.: Harcourt, Brace & Co., 1999.

Coil, Suzanne M. *Mardi Gras*. New York: Macmillan, 1994.

Fontenot, Mary Alice. *Mardi Gras in the Country*. Gretna, La.: Pelican Publishing Co., 1995.

Gabbert, Lisa. *Mardi Gras: A City's Masked Parade*. Center City, Minn.: Powerkids Press, 1999.

Goldsmith, Diane Hoyt. *Mardi Gras: A Cajun Country Celebration*. New York: Holiday House, 1995.

# Internet Addresses

★

INFOPLEASE: MARDI GRAS
<http://www.infoplease.com/spot/
    mardigras1.html>

MARDI GRAS ON THE NET
<http://www.holidays.net/mardigras/>

MARDI GRAS
<http://www.mardigras.org>

# Index

★